AWS Certified Cloud Practitioner

Exam Practice Questions

www.ipspecialist.net

[Document Control]

Proposal Name	:	AWS CCP – Practice Questions
Document Version	:	1.0
Document Release Date	:	22 May 2018
Reference	:	CLF-C01

Feedback:

If you have any comments regarding the quality of this book, or otherwise alter it to better suit your needs, you can contact us through email at info@ipspecialist.net

Please make sure to include the book title and ISBN in your message.

About IPSpecialist

IPSPECIALIST LTD. IS COMMITTED TO EXCELLENCE AND DEDICATED TO YOUR SUCCESS.

Our philosophy is to treat our customers like family. We want you to succeed, and we are willing to do anything possible to help you make it happen. We have the proof to back up our claims. We strive to accelerate billions of careers with great courses, accessibility, and affordability. We believe that continuous learning and knowledge evolution are most important things to keep re-skilling and up-skilling the world.

Planning and creating a specific goal is where IPSpecialist helps. We can create a career track that suits your visions as well as develop the competencies you need to become a professional Network Engineer. We can also assist you with the execution and evaluation of proficiency level based on the career track you choose, as they are customized to fit your specific goals.

We help you STAND OUT from the crowd through our detailed IP training content packages.

Course Features:

- *Self-Paced learning*
    - O Learn at your own pace and in your own time
- *Covers Complete Exam Blueprint*
    - O Prep-up for the exam with confidence
- *Case Study Based Learning*
    - O Relate the content to real-life scenarios
- *Subscriptions that suits you*
    - O Get more pay less with IPS Subscriptions
- *Career Advisory Services*
    - O Let industry experts plan your career journey
- *Virtual Labs to test your skills*
    - O With IPS vRacks, you can testify your exam preparations
- *Practice Questions*
    - O Practice Questions to measure your preparation standards
- *On Request Digital Certification*
    - O On request, digital certification from IPSpecialist LTD.

About the Authors:

This book has been compiled with the help of multiple professional engineers. These engineers specialize in different fields, e.g., Networking, Security, Cloud, Big Data, IoT, etc. Each engineer develops content in its specialized field that is compiled to form a comprehensive certification guide.

About the Technical Reviewers:

Nouman Ahmed Khan

AWS-Architect, CCDE, CCIEX5 (R&S, SP, Security, DC, Wireless), CISSP, CISA, CISM is a Solution Architect working with a major telecommunication provider in Qatar. He works with enterprises, mega-projects, and service providers to help them select the best-fit technology solutions. He also works closely as a consultant to understand customer business processes and helps select an appropriate technology strategy to support business goals. He has more than 14 years of experience working in Pakistan/Middle-East & UK. He holds a Bachelor of Engineering Degree from NED University, Pakistan, and M.Sc. in Computer Networks from the UK.

Abubakar Saeed

Abubakar Saeed has more than twenty-five years of experience, Managing, Consulting, Designing, and implementing large-scale technology projects, extensive experience heading ISP operations, solutions integration, heading Product Development, Presales, and Solution Design. Emphasizing on adhering to Project timelines and delivering as per customer expectations, he always leads the project in the right direction with his innovative ideas and excellent management.

Muhammad Yousuf

Muhammad Yousuf is a professional technical content writer. He is Cisco Certified Network Associate in Routing and Switching, holding bachelor's degree in Telecommunication Engineering from Sir Syed University of Engineering and Technology. He has both technical knowledge and industry sounding information, which he uses perfectly in his career.

Saima Talat

Saima Talat is a postgraduate Computer Engineer working professionally as a Technical Content Developer. She is a part of a team of professionals operating in the E-learning and digital education sector. She holds a bachelor's degree in Computer Engineering accompanied by Masters of Engineering in Computer Networks and Performance Evaluation from NED University, Pakistan. With strong educational background, she possesses exceptional researching and writing skills that have led her to impart knowledge through her professional career.

Table of Contents

About this Book

This book 'IPSpecialist's AWS Certified Cloud Practitioner Practice Questions' is a part of the IPSpecialist's AWS Certified Cloud Practitioner Exam training course series. These Practice Questions are specifically designed from the exam perspective to help you evaluate your preparation. The series includes 'IPSpecialist's AWS Certified Cloud Practitioner Technology Workbook', which provides in-depth understanding and complete course material to pass the AWS Certified Cloud Practitioner Exam (CLF-C01). Apart from the Technology Workbook and Practice Questions, the series also include 'IPSpecialist's AWS Certified Cloud Practitioner Quick Reference Sheet'. The training course is designed to take a practical approach to learning with real-life examples and case studies.

AWS Cloud Certification:

AWS Certifications are industry-recognized credentials that validate your technical cloud skills and expertise while assisting in your career growth. These are one of the most valuable IT certifications right now since AWS has established an overwhelming lead in the public cloud market. Even with the presence of several tough competitors such as Microsoft Azure, Google Cloud Engine, and Rackspace, AWS is by far the dominant public cloud platform today, with an astounding collection of proprietary services that continues to grow.

The two key reasons as to why AWS certifications are prevailing in the current cloud-oriented job market:

- There's a dire need for skilled cloud engineers, developers, and architects – and the current shortage of experts is expected to continue into the foreseeable future.
- AWS certifications stand out for their thoroughness, rigour, consistency, and appropriateness for critical cloud engineering positions.

Value of AWS Certifications

AWS places equal emphasis on sound conceptual knowledge of its entire platform, as well as on hands-on experience with the AWS infrastructure and its many unique and complex components and services.

For Individuals

- Demonstrate your expertise to design, deploy, and operate highly available, cost-effective, and secure applications on AWS
- Gain recognition and visibility for your proven skills and proficiency with AWS
- Earn tangible benefits such as access to the AWS Certified LinkedIn Community, invite to AWS Certification Appreciation Receptions and Lounges, AWS Certification Practice Exam Voucher, Digital Badge for certification validation, AWS Certified Logo usage, access to AWS Certified Store
- Foster credibility with your employer and peers

For Employers

- Identify skilled professionals to lead IT initiatives with AWS technologies
- Reduce risks and costs to implement your workloads and projects on the AWS platform
- Increase customer satisfaction

Types of Certification

Role-Based Certifications:

- *Foundational* - Validates overall understanding of the AWS Cloud. Prerequisite to achieving Specialty certification or an optional start towards Associate certification.
- *Associate* - Technical role-based certifications. No prerequisite.
- *Professional* - Highest level technical role-based certification. Relevant Associate certification required.

Specialty Certifications:

- Validate advanced skills in specific technical areas
- Requires one active role-based certification

Certification Roadmap

AWS Certified Cloud Practitioner is a new entry-level certification. Furthermore, there are five different AWS certification offerings in three different tracks which include Solutions Architect, Developer and SysOps Administrator. AWS also offers two specialty certifications in technical areas which are Big Data and Advanced Networking.

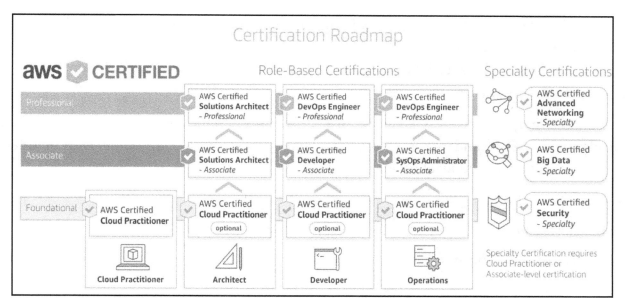

Figure 1. Certification Roadmap

AWS Certified Cloud Practitioner

The AWS Certified Cloud Practitioner (CLF-C01) examination is intended for individuals who have the knowledge and skills necessary to effectively demonstrate an overall understanding of the AWS Cloud, independent of specific technical roles addressed by other AWS certifications (e.g., Solutions Architect - Associate, Developer - Associate, or SysOps Administrator - Associate). This exam enables individuals to validate their knowledge of the AWS Cloud with an industry-recognized credential.

Overview of AWS Cloud Practitioner Certification

This exam certifies an individual's ability & understanding of the following:

- AWS Cloud and its basic global infrastructure
- Basic AWS Cloud architectural principles
- AWS Cloud value proposition
- Key services on the AWS platform and their common use cases (e.g., compute, analytics, etc.)
- Basic security and compliance aspects of the AWS platform and the shared security model
- Billing, account management, and pricing models

- Identify sources of documentation or technical assistance (example, white papers or support tickets)
- Basic/Core characteristics of deploying and operating in the AWS Cloud

Intended Audience

Candidates may be business analysts, project managers, chief experience officers, AWS Academy students, and other IT-related professionals. They may be serving in sales, marketing, finance, and legal roles.

Exam Details

Pricing: USD 100

Exam Length: 90 minutes

Exam Content: Two types of questions on the examination

- Multiple-choice: Has one correct response and three incorrect responses (distractors).
- Multiple-response: Has two correct responses out of five options.

Always choose the best response(s). Incorrect responses will be plausible and are designed to be attractive to candidates who do not know the correct response. Unanswered questions are scored as incorrect. There is no penalty for guessing.

Exam Results:

The AWS Certified Cloud Practitioner (CLF-C01) examination is a pass or fail exam. The examination is scored against a minimum standard established by AWS professionals who are guided by certification industry best practices and guidelines.

The results of the examination are reported as a scaled score from 100 through 1000, with a minimum passing score of 700. The score shows how you performed on the examination as a whole and whether or not you passed.

Exam Validity: 2 years; Recertification is required every 2 years for all AWS Certifications.

How to become an AWS Certified Cloud Practitioner?

Prerequisites

No prerequisite exam is required. Although it is recommended to have at least six months of AWS cloud experience in any role, including technical, managerial, sales, purchasing,

or financial. Also, the candidates should have a basic understanding of IT services and their uses in the AWS Cloud platform.

Exam Preparation Guide

Exam preparation can be accomplished through self-study with textbooks, practice exams, and on-site classroom programs. This workbook provides you with all the information and knowledge to help you pass the AWS Certified Cloud Practitioner Exam. IPSpecialist provides full support to the candidates in order for them to pass the exam.

Step 1: Take AWS Training Class

These training courses and materials will help with exam preparation:

AWS Training (aws.amazon.com/training)

- AWS Cloud Practitioner Essentials course

- AWS Technical Essentials course

- AWS Business Essentials course

Step 2: Review the Exam Guide and Sample Questions

Review the Exam Blue Print and study the Sample Questions available at AWS website

Step 3: Practice with Self-Paced Labs and Study Official Documentations

Register for an AWS Free Tier account to use limited free services and practice Labs. Additionally, you can study official documentation on the website

Step 4: Study AWS Whitepapers

Broaden your technical understanding with whitepapers written by the AWS team.

AWS Whitepapers (aws.amazon.com/whitepapers) Kindle, .pdf and Other Materials

- Overview of Amazon Web Services whitepaper, April 2017

- Architecting for the Cloud: AWS Best Practices whitepaper, Feb 2016

- How AWS Pricing Works whitepaper, March 2016

- The Total Cost of (Non) Ownership of Web Applications in the Cloud whitepaper, Aug 2012

- Compare AWS Support Plans webpage

Step 5: Review AWS FAQs

Browse through these FAQs to find answers to commonly raised questions.

Step 6: Take a Practice Exam

Test your knowledge online in a timed environment by registering at aws.training.

Step 7: Schedule Your Exam and Get Certified

Schedule your exam at a testing center near you at aws.training.

Chapter 1: Cloud Concepts

Q1. What is the pricing model that allows AWS customers to pay for resources on an as needed basis?

    a. Pay as you go
    b. Pay as you own
    c. Pay as you reserve
    d. Pay as you use
    e. Pay as you buy

Q2. Which of the following are NOT benefits of AWS cloud computing? (Choose 2)

    a. Fault tolerant databases
    b. High latency
    c. Multiple procurement cycles
    d. Temporary and disposable resources
    e. High availability

Q3. Which of the following is NOT an advantage of cloud computing over on-premise computing?

    a. Benefit from massive economies of scale
    b. Trade capital expense for variable expense
    c. Pay for racking, stacking, and powering servers
    d. Eliminate guessing on your infrastructure capacity needs
    e. Increase speed and agility

Q4. What is the one main reason customers are switching to cloud computing?

    a. Finite infrastructure
    b. Automation
    c. Overprovisioning
    d. Instant configuration
    e. Agility

Q5. Which of the following are advantages of cloud computing? (Choose 4)

a. The ability to 'go global' in minutes
b. Increased speed and agility
c. Variable expense
d. Requires large amounts of capital
e. Elasticity – you need not worry about capacity

Q6. Which of the following are characteristics of cloud computing? (Choose 3)

a. Cloud charges are capital expenditures
b. Pay-as-you-go pricing
c. On-demand delivery
d. Services are delivered via the Internet

Q7. Which of the following are types of cloud computing deployments? (Choose 3)

a. Public cloud
b. Hybrid cloud
c. Mixed cloud
d. Private cloud

Q8. Amazon Lightsail is an example of which of the following?

a. Software as a Service
b. Platform as a Service
c. Functions as a Service
d. Infrastructure as a Service

Q9. Which of the following are principles of sound cloud design? (Choose 4)

a. Disposable resources
b. Infrastructure as code
c. Assume *everything* will fail
d. Limit the number of 3rd-party services
e. Scalability
f. Tightly-coupled components
g. Treat your servers like pets, not cattle

Q10. Which AWS service allows you to run code without having to worry about provisioning any underlying resources (such as virtual machines, databases etc.)

a. EC2
b. DynamoDB
c. EC2 Container Service
d. Lambda

Q11. When considering cost optimization, what model allows you to pay only for what computing resources you actually use?

a. Economies of scale model
b. Expenditure model
c. Economies of scope model
d. Consumption model

Q12. What is defined as the ability for a system to remain operational even if some of the components of that system fail?

a. High durability
b. DNS failovers
c. High availability
d. Fault tolerance

Q13. What tool helps avoid limitations of being able to create new resources on-demand or scheduled?

a. CloudWatch
b. Route 53
c. Auto Scaling
d. Elastic Load Balancer

Q14. Which of the following is NOT one of the four areas of the performance efficiency pillar?

a. Selection
b. Tradeoffs
c. Traceability
d. Monitoring

Q15. Which design principles are recommended when considering performance efficiency? (Choose 2)

a. Serverless architecture
b. Expenditure awareness
c. Matching supply with demand
d. Enabling traceability
e. Democratize advanced technologies

Q16. Why is AWS more economical than traditional data centers for applications with varying compute workloads?

a. Amazon Elastic Compute Cloud (Amazon EC2) costs are billed on a monthly basis.
b. Customers retain full administrative access to their Amazon EC2 instances.
c. Amazon EC2 instances can be launched on-demand when needed.
d. Customers can permanently run enough instances to handle peak workloads.

Chapter 2: Security

Q1. Which of the following are advantages of AWS cloud security? (Choose 2)

    a. AWS uses single-factor access control systems
    b. AWS retains complete control and ownership of your data region
    c. AWS infrastructure security auditing is periodic and manual
    d. AWS uses multi-factor access control systems
    e. You retain complete control and ownership of your data region

Q2. Which of the following are steps you should take in securing your Root AWS account? (Choose 3)

    a. Create a Root IAM role.
    b. Create individual IAM users.
    c. Activate Multifactor Authentication (MFA) on your root account.
    d. Use roles to assign permissions to IAM users.

Q3. Which of the following is the document used to grant permissions to users, groups, and roles?

    a. Policy
    b. Passbook
    c. Protocol
    d. Paradigm

Q4. IAM policies are written using _____.

    a. XML
    b. SAML
    c. JSON
    d. SGML

Q5. Which of the following are valid access types for an IAM user? (Choose 3)

    a. Using the AWS Software Developers Kit
    b. Emergency access via Identity Access Management (IAM)
    c. AWS Management Console access

d. Programmatic access via the command line

e. Security Group access via the AWS command line

Q6. Which of the following Compliance certifications attests to the security of the AWS platform regarding credit card transactions?

a. ISO 27001

b. SOC 2

c. SOC 1

d. PCI DSS Level 1

Q7. Which of the following is AWS' managed DDoS protection service?

a. AWS Shield

b. Security Groups

c. AWS WAF

d. Access Control Lists

Q8. Which of the following AWS services can help you assess the fault-tolerance of your AWS environment?

a. AWS WAF

b. AWS Trusted Advisor

c. AWS Shield

d. AWS Inspector

Q9. The AWS Web Application Firewall can go down to which of the following OSI layers?

a. 4

b. 5

c. 6

d. 7

Q10. You need to use an AWS service to assess the security and compliance of your EC2 instances. Which of the following services should you use?

a. AWS WAF

b. AWS Inspector

c. AWS Shield

d. AWS Trusted Advisor

Q11. Which of the following Compliance guarantees attests to the fact that the AWS Platform has met the standard required for the secure storage of medical records in the US?

a. HIPPA
b. FERPA
c. GLBA
d. HITECH

Q12. Which of the following services will help you optimize your entire AWS environment in real time following AWS best practices?

a. AWS WAF
b. AWS Trusted Advisor
c. AWS Shield
d. AWS Inspector

Q13. You need to implement an automated service that will scan your AWS environment with the goal of both improving security and reducing costs. Which service should you use?

a. Service Catalog
b. CloudTrail
c. Trusted Advisor
d. Config Rules

Q14. Which of the following AWS services can assist you with cost optimization?

a. AWS WAF
b. AWS Trusted Advisor
c. AWS Inspector
d. AWS Shield

Q15. Under the Shared Responsibility model, for which of the following does AWS not assume responsibility?

a. Physical security of AWS facilities
b. Networking

    c. Customer data

    d. Hypervisors

Q16. Which of the following is true about security groups? (Choose 2)

    a. Acts as a virtual firewall to control outbound traffic only

    b. All inbound traffic is denied and outbound traffic is allowed by default

    c. Acts as a virtual firewall to control inbound and outbound traffic

    d. Acts as a virtual firewall to control inbound traffic only

    e. All inbound traffic is allowed and outbound traffic is denied by default

Q17. Which of the following is NOT a feature of AWS Identity and Access Management?

    a. Manage roles and their permissions

    b. Manage users and their access

    c. Manage federated users and their permissions

    d. Manage services and their capacities

Q18. What is AWS Trusted Advisor?

    a. Partner program that helps you validate your application deployment

    b. Online tool that helps you configure resources to follow best practices

    c. Professional Services offering that helps you migrate to cloud

    d. AWS service that helps you manage access to your account

Q19. When creating an IAM policy, what are the two types of access that can be granted to a user? (Choose 2)

    a. Authorized Access

    b. AWS Management Console Access

    c. Institutional Access

    d. Programmatic Access

    e. Administrative Root Access

Q20. Which of the following are the security benefits that AWS offers? (Choose 2)

    a. Secure Global Infrastructure

    b. Meet compliance requirements

    c. Shared Collaboration Model

    d. Data Storage

e. Inventory and Application Management

Q21. The AWS Risk and Compliance Program is made up of which of the following components? (Choose 3)

a. Security Principles
b. Risk Management
c. Control Environment
d. Information Security
e. Physical Security
f. Automation Environment
g. Identity Management

Q22. What does AWS recommend as the best practice for the AWS Account Root User after initial login?

a. Delete root user account
b. Delete root user access keys
c. Revoke all permissions on root user account
d. Restrict permissions on root user account

Q23. In the Shared Responsibility Model, which of the following are an example of "Security in the cloud"? (Choose 2)

a. Compliance with computer security standards and regulations
b. Physical security of the facilities in which the services operate
c. Which AWS services are used with the content
d. Protecting the global infrastructure
e. In which country the content is stored

Q24. Which of the following are included in AWS Assurance Programs (Choose 2)

a. Laws, Regulations, and Privacy
b. Customer Testimonials
c. Partner Validations
d. Industry Best Practices
e. Certification/Attestations

Q25. In the Shared Responsibility Model, for which aspect of securing the cloud is AWS responsible?

   a. Security of the cloud
   b. Security to the cloud
   c. Security for the cloud
   d. Security in the cloud

Q26. Which of the following are resources that AWS provides to customers as guidance to secure their data in the cloud? (Choose 2)

   a. Customer Testimonials
   b. AWS Security Learning Path
   c. AWS Enterprise Support
   d. AWS Trusted Advisor
   e. Certified Partner Solutions

Q27. In a physical data center, security is typically considered in what area?

   a. Only in the perimeter
   b. In an edge location
   c. In the closest region
   d. In the closest availability zones

Q28. Which of the following is NOT considered a fault tolerant tool?

   a. S3
   b. SQS
   c. WAF
   d. RD

Q29. Which of the following cloud security controls ensures that only authorized and authenticated users are able to access your resources?

   a. Detective controls
   b. Identity and Access Management
   c. Infrastructure protection
   d. Incident response

Q30. Which of the following is AWS's responsibility under the AWS shared responsibility model?

    a. Configuring third-party applications
    b. Maintaining physical hardware
    c. Securing application access and data
    d. Managing custom Amazon Machine Images (AMIs)

Q31. How would a system administrator add an additional layer of login security to a user's AWS Management Console?

    a. Use AWS Cloud Directory
    b. Audit AWS Identity and Access Management (IAM) roles
    c. Enable Multi-Factor Authentication
    d. Enable AWS CloudTrail

Q32. True or False: It is safer to use Access Keys than it is to use IAM roles.

    a. True
    b. False

Q33. True or False: Identity Access Management (IAM) is a Regional service.

    a. True
    b. False

Q34. True or False: Security in the cloud is the responsibility of AWS.

    a. True
    b. False

Q35. True or False: The Standard version of AWS Shield offers automated application (layer 7) traffic monitoring.

    a. True
    b. False

Chapter 3: Technology

Q1. Which of the following AWS tools help your application scale up or down based on demand? (Choose 2)

    a. Agile Load Balancing
    b. Elastic Load Balancing
    c. Auto Availability Zones
    d. AWS CloudFormation
    e. Auto Scaling

Q2. What is true about Regions? (Choose 2)

    a. Each region is located in a separate geographic area
    b. All regions are located in one specific geographic area
    c. Physical location of your customers
    d. Physical location with multiple Availability Zones
    e. Resources are replicated across all regions by default

Q3. Which of the following best describes Availability Zones?

    a. Restricted areas designed specifically for the creation of Virtual Private Clouds.
    b. Distinct locations from within an AWS region that are engineered to be isolated from failures.
    c. A Content Distribution Network used to deliver content to users.
    d. Two zones containing compute resources that are designed to automatically maintain synchronized copies of each other's data.

Q4. Which of the following is correct?

    a. # of Regions > # of Availability Zones > # of Edge Locations
    b. # of Edge Locations > # of Availability Zones > # of Regions
    c. # of Availability Zones > # of Edge Locations > # of Regions
    d. # of Availability Zones > # of Regions > # of Edge Locations

Q5. Which of the following data archival services is extremely inexpensive, but has a 3-5 hour data-retrieval window?

a. S3-RRS
b. S3
c. Glacier
d. S3-IA

Q6. Which of the following best describes EBS?

a. A NoSQL database service
b. A managed database service
c. A virtual hard-disk in the cloud
d. A bitcoin-mining service

Q7. Which of the following EC2 options is best for long-term workloads with predictable usage patterns?

a. Reserved instances
b. Dedicated Host
c. Spot instances
d. On-Demand instances

Q8. In which of the following is CloudFront content cached?

a. Data Center
b. Edge Location
c. Region
d. Availability Zone

Q9. Which of the following best describes an AWS Region?

a. A collection of databases that can only be accessed from a specific geographic region.
b. A console that gives you a quick, global picture of your cloud computing environment.
c. A distinct location within a geographic area designed to provide high availability to a specific geography.
d. A collection of data centers that is spread evenly around a specific continent.

Q10. There are at least _____ Availability Zones per AWS Region.

a. 2

b. 4

c. 1

d. 3

Q11. Which of the following best describes a Resource Group?

  a. A resource group is a collection of resources that share one or more tags (or portions of tags.)
  b. A resource group is a collection of resources of the same type (EC2, S3, etc.) that are deployed in the same Availability Zone.
  c. A resource group is a collection of resources of the same type (EC2, S3, etc.) that share one or more tags or portions of tags.
  d. A resource group is a collection of resources that are deployed in the same AWS Region.

Q12. Which of the following are valid EC2 pricing options? (Choose 2)

  a. On-Demand
  b. Stop
  c. Reserved
  d. Enterprise

Q13. Which AWS service is specifically designed to assist you in processing large data sets?

  a. EMR
  b. EC2
  c. AWS Big Data Processing
  d. ElastiCache

Q14. You have a mission-critical application which must be globally available at all times. Which deployment strategy should you follow?

  a. Multi-Availability Zone
  b. Multi-VPC in two AWS Regions
  c. Multi-Region
  d. Deploy to all Availability Zones in your home region.

Q15. You need to host a file in a location that's publicly accessible from anywhere in the world. Which AWS service would best meet that need?

    a. S3
    b. EBS
    c. RDS
    d. EC2

Q16. Which of the following is AWS' managed database service that is up to 5X faster than a traditional MySQL database.

    a. MariaDB
    b. PostgreSQL
    c. DynamoDB
    d. Aurora

Q17. What is an AWS region?

    a. A region is an independent data center, located in different countries around the globe.
    b. A region is a subset of AWS technologies. For example, the Compute region consists of EC2, ECS, Lambda, etc.
    c. A region is a collection of Edge Locations available in specific countries.
    d. A region is a geographical area divided into Availability Zones. Each region contains at least two Availability Zones.

Q18. Which of the following is AWS' Data Warehousing service?

    a. Snowball
    b. Elastic Map Reduce
    c. S3 Big Data
    d. Redshift

Q19. Which of the following are AWS compute services? (Choose 2)

    a. EC2
    b. Lambda
    c. EBS
    d. SNS

Q20. Which of the following AWS services should you use to migrate an existing database to AWS?

    a. Route 53
    b. Storage Gateway
    c. DMS
    d. SNS

Q21. Which of the following is NOT an AWS Region?

    a. Frankfurt
    b. Ireland
    c. Oregon
    d. Virginia
    e. Moscow

Q22. Which of the following statements are true about Availability Zones? (Choose 2)

    a. Multiple zones will fail if one zone fails
    b. Multiple zones are connected by low latency network links
    c. A single zone equals a single data center
    d. Multiple zones are physically connected on the same grid
    e. A single zone can span multiple data centers

Q23. What AWS tool utilizes edge locations to cache content and reduce latency?

    a. RDS
    b. EBS Storage
    c. EC2 Instances
    d. AWS CloudFront
    e. VPC's

Q24. How does an edge location help end users?

    a. Increases latency
    b. Reduces scaling
    c. Increases storage
    d. Reduces latency
    e. Reduces power consumption

Q25. Which of the following describes Elastic Load Balancers (ELB)?

    a. Translates domain names into IP addresses

    b. Creates new resources on-demand

    c. Launches or terminates instances based on specific conditions

    d. Distributes incoming traffic amongst your instances

Q26. Which of the following are high availability characteristics of Amazon Route 53? (Choose 2)

    a. Latency-based routing

    b. Geolocation routing

    c. Terminate instances based on specified conditions

    d. Mask failure of an instance/software

    e. Collect and track high latency metrics

Q27. What type of applications are recommended for Amazon EC2 reserved instances?

    a. Applications being developed or tested for the first time

    b. Applications that are only feasible at lower compute prices

    c. Applications that have flexible start and end times

    d. Applications with steady state or predictable usage

Q28. Which AWS service would simplify migration of a database to AWS?

    a. AWS Storage Gateway

    b. AWS Database Migration Service (AWS DMS)

    c. Amazon Elastic Compute Cloud (Amazon EC2)

    d. Amazon AppStream 2.0

Q29. Which AWS offering enables customers to find, buy, and immediately start using software solutions in their AWS environment?

    a. AWS Config

    b. AWS OpsWorks

    c. AWS SDK

    d. AWS Marketplace

Q30. Which AWS networking service enables a company to create a virtual network within AWS?

a. AWS Config
b. Amazon Route 53
c. AWS Direct Connect
d. Amazon Virtual Private Cloud (Amazon VPC)

Q31. Which component of AWS global infrastructure does Amazon CloudFront use to ensure low-latency delivery?

a. AWS Regions
b. AWS edge locations
c. AWS Availability Zones
d. Amazon Virtual Private Cloud (Amazon VPC)

Q32. Which service can identify the user that made the API call when an Amazon Elastic Compute Cloud (Amazon EC2) instance is terminated?

a. Amazon CloudWatch
b. AWS CloudTrail
c. AWS X-Ray
d. AWS Identity and Access Management (AWS IAM)

Q33. Which service would you use to send alerts based on Amazon CloudWatch alarms?

a. Amazon Simple Notification Service (Amazon SNS)
b. AWS CloudTrail
c. AWS Trusted Advisor
d. Amazon Route 53

Q34. Where can a customer find information about prohibited actions on AWS infrastructure?

a. AWS Trusted Advisor
b. AWS Identity and Access Management (IAM)
c. AWS Billing Console
d. AWS Acceptable Use Policy

Q35. True or False: S3 is object storage suitable for the storage of 'flat' files like Word documents, photos, etc.

a. True

b. False

Q36. True or False: To restrict access to an entire bucket, you use bucket control lists; and to restrict access to an individual object, you use object policies.

    a. True

    b. False

Q37. True or False: S3 can be used to host a dynamic website, like one that runs on a LAMP stack.

    a. True

    b. False

Q38. True or False: A Distribution is what we call a series of Edge Locations that make up CDN.

    a. True

    b. False

Q39. True or False: There are more Regions than there are Availability Zones.

    a. True

    b. False

Q40. True or False: Objects stored in S3 are stored in a single, central location within AWS.

    a. True

    b. False

Q41. True or False: Both you and a friend can have an S3 bucket called 'mytestbucket'.

    a. True

    b. False

Q42. True or False: A CloudFront Origin can be an S3 bucket, an EC2 instance, an Elastic Load Balancer, or Route 53.

    a. True

b. False

Q43. True or False: S3 Transfer Acceleration uses AWS' network of Availability Zones to more quickly get your data into AWS.

a. True
b. False

Q44. True or False: Access Control Lists are used to make entire buckets (like one hosting an S3 website) public.

a. True
b. False

Chapter 4: Billing and Pricing

Q1. Which of the following AWS Support levels offers 24x7 support via phone or chat?

   a. Developer
   b. Business
   c. Basic
   d. Individual

Q2. Which of the following are Support Levels offered by AWS? (Choose 3)

   a. Start-up
   b. Individual
   c. Basic
   d. Developer
   e. Business

Q3. Which of the following AWS Support levels offers the assistance of a Technical Account Manager?

   a. Business
   b. Developer
   c. Elite
   d. Enterprise

Q4. By default, what is the maximum number of Linked Accounts per Paying Account under Consolidated Billing?

   a. 10
   b. 20
   c. 50
   d. 100

Q5. Which of the following support plans features access to AWS support during business hours via email?

a. Basic
b. Developer
c. Business
d. Enterprise

Q6. Which of the following EC2 instance types will realize a savings over time in exchange for a contracted term-of-service?

a. Spot instances
b. On-demand instances
c. Discount instances
d. Reserved instances

Q7. Which of the following AWS services are free to use? (Choose 5)

a. VPC
b. S3
c. Route 53
d. RDS
e. Auto-Scaling
f. Elastic Beanstalk
g. CloudFormation
h. EBS
i. EC2
j. IAM

Q8. Which of the following support plans features a < 4-hour response time in the event of an impaired production system?

a. Individual
b. Basic
c. Developer
d. Business

Q9. Which of the following are criteria affecting your billing for RDS? (Choose 3)

a. Additional storage
b. Data transfer in
c. Standby time

    d. Clock hours of server time

    e. Number of requests

Q10. Which of the following is not a fundamental AWS charge?

    a. Data-in

    b. Compute

    c. Data-out

    d. Storage

Q11. Which of the following AWS services should you use if you'd like to be notified when you have crossed a billing threshold?

    a. CloudWatch

    b. AWS Bugdet

    c. AWS Cost Allocation

    d. Trusted Advisor

Q12. Which of the following support services do all accounts receive as standard?

    a. Technical support

    b. Billing support

    c. 24/7 support via phone and chat

    d. Technical Account Manager

Q13. Your Development team uses four on-demand EC2 instances and your QA team has 5 reserved instances, only three of which are being used. Assuming all AWS accounts are under a single AWS Organization, how will the Development team's instances be billed?

    a. All the Dev instances will be billed at the reserved instance rate.

    b. The pricing for the reserved instances will shift from QA to Dev.

    c. All the Dev team's instances will be billed at the on-demand rate.

    d. The Dev team will be billed for two instances at on-demand prices and two instances at the reserved instance price.

Q14. Which of the following support plans features unlimited (customer-side) contacts and unlimited support cases? (Choose 2)

    a. Developer

    b. Business

c. Enterprise

d. Basic

Q15. You have a project that will require 90 hours of computing time. There is no deadline, and the work can be stopped and restarted without adverse effect. Which of the following computing options offers the most cost-effective solution?

a. Spot instances

b. ECS instances

c. On-demand instances

d. Reserved instances

Q16. When calculating the cost of Amazon EC2, what factors affect pricing? (Choose 2)

a. Number and size of objects stored in your Amazon S3 buckets

b. Number of hours Elastic Load Balancer runs

c. Number of items in your inbound data transfer

d. Number of instances

Q17. Which of the following is NOT included in the AWS Free Tier?

a. AWS CloudFormation

b. AWS Identity and Access Management (IAM)

c. AWS Web Application Firewall (WAF)

d. Amazon Virtual Private Cloud (VPC)

e. Amazon Simple Storage Service (S3)

Q18. What AWS tool compares the cost of running your application in an on-premise data center to AWS?

a. Total Cost of Operation (TCO) calculator

b. Total Cost of Products (TCP) calculator

c. Total Cost of Services (TCS) calculator

d. Total Cost of Application (TCA) calculator

e. Total Cost of Ownership (TCO) calculator

Q19. What is NOT a consideration when estimating the cost of Amazon S3?

a. Number and size of objects

b. Input Output Operations per Seconds (IOPS)

c. Storage class
d. Data transfer
e. Requests

Q20. Which of the following is NOT available in the Business Support Plan?

a. Access to Infrastructure Event Management
b. Access to third-party software support
c. Access to Cloud Support Engineers for technical issues
d. Access to Well-Architected Review delivered by AWS Solution Architects
e. Access to Personal Health Dashboard and Health API

Q21. What are the characteristics of the Developer Support Plan? (Choose 2)

a. Assigned to a Technical Account Manager
b. Unlimited contacts may open a case
c. 24/7 access to Cloud Support Engineers via email, chat, and phone
d. One primary contact may open a case
e. Business hours access to Cloud Support Associates via email

Q22. As AWS grows, the general cost of doing business is reduced and savings are passed back to the customer in the form of lower pricing. What is this cost optimization called?

a. Economies of scale
b. Economies of optimization
c. Economies of scope
d. Economies of cost
e. Economies of labor

Q23. What type of AWS data transfers are free? (Choose 2)

a. Inbound data transfer across all Amazon Web Services in all regions
b. Inbound data transfer between Amazon Web Services within the same region
c. Outbound data transfer across all Amazon Web Services in all regions
d. Outbound data transfer from S3 only
e. Outbound data transfer between Amazon Web Services within the same region

Q24. True or False: With Consolidated Billing, the Paying Account can make changes to any of the resources owned by a Linked Account.

a. True

b. False

Q25. True or False: With AWS Organizations, you can use either just the Consolidated Billing feature, or all the offered features.

a. True

b. False

Answers

Chapter 1: Cloud Concepts

1. **A** (Pay as you go)

Explanation:

AWS offers you a pay-as-you-go approach for pricing for over 70 cloud services.

2. **B** (High latency)

    C (Multiple procurement cycles)

Explanation:

AWS network offers performance (high bandwidth, low latency) and scalability. AWS provides an efficient cloud-centric procurement process.

3. **C** (Pay for racking, stacking, and powering servers)

Explanation:

The six advantages are:
    1. Trade capital expense for variable expense
    2. Benefit from massive economies of scale
    3. Stop guessing capacity
    4. Increase speed and agility
    5. Stop spending money on running and maintaining data centers
    6. Go global in minutes

4. **E** (Agility)

Explanation:

Increased agility, elasticity, focus on core business, optimized costs, and better security are all good outcomes when it comes to working with AWS.

5. **A** (The ability to 'go global' in minutes)

    B (Increased speed and agility)

    C (Variable expense)

    E (Elasticity – you need not worry about capacity)

Explanation:

The 'pay-as-you-go' nature of cloud computing ensures that a large up-front capital expense is not required

6. **B** (Pay-as-you-go pricing)

    C (On-demand delivery)

    D (Services are delivered via the Internet)

Explanation:

Services incurred from a cloud services provider are operating expenses, not capital expenses. The other answers are correct.

7. **A** (Public cloud)
    B (Hybrid cloud)
    D (Private cloud)

Explanation:

The three types of cloud deployments are Public, Hybrid, and Private (On-premises).

8. **B** (Platform as a Service)

Explanation:

Lightsail is AWS' Platform-as-a-Service offering.

9. **A** (Disposable resources)
    B (Infrastructure as code)

C (Assume *everything* will fail)

E (Scalability)

Explanation:

Build your systems to be scalable, use disposable resources, reduce infrastructure to code, and, please, assume EVERYTHING will fail sooner or later.

10. **D** (Lambda)

Explanation:

Lambda is the AWS Function-as-a-Service (FaaS) offering that lets you run code without provisioning or managing servers.

11. **D** (Consumption model)

Explanation:

With AWS you only pay for the services you consume

12. **D** (Fault tolerance)

Explanation:

Fault tolerance is the ability of a system to remain operational even if some of the components of the system fail

13. **C** (Auto Scaling)

Explanation:

AWS Auto Scaling monitors your application and automatically adds or removes capacity from your resource groups in real-time as demands change.

14. **C** (Traceability)

Explanation:

Performance efficiency in the cloud is composed of four areas:

1. Selection

2. Review

3. Monitoring

4. Trade-offs

15. **A** (Serverless architecture)

    E (Democratize advanced technologies)

Explanation:

Performance Efficiency principles are:

1. Democratize advanced technologies

2. Go global in minutes

3. Use serverless architectures

4. Experiment more often

5. Mechanical sympathy

16. **C** (Amazon EC2 instances can be launched on-demand when needed)

Explanation:

The ability to launch instances on-demand when needed allows customers launch and terminate instances in response to a varying workload. This is a more economical practice than purchasing enough on-premises servers to handle the peak load.

Chapter 2: Security

1. **D** (AWS uses multi-factor access control systems)

   E (You retain complete control and ownership of your data region)

Explanation:

AWS uses Multi-Factor Authentication that adds an extra layer of protection on top of your user name and password. AWS manages security of the cloud, while security in the cloud is the responsibility of the customer.

2. **B** (Create individual IAM users)

   C (Activate Multifactor Authentication (MFA) on your root account)

   D (Use roles to assign permissions to IAM users)

Explanation:

The Root account should have MFA enabled; you should always create individual users (the Root account should never be used for actual work); and roles should be used to grant permissions to the users you create.

3. **A** (Policy)

Explanation:

A Policy is the document used to grant permissions to users, groups, and roles.

4. **C** (JSON)

Explanation:

IAM policies are written using JSON.

5. **A** (Using the AWS Software Developers Kit)

   C (AWS Management Console access)

   D (Programmatic access via the command line)

Explanation:

The two types of access are AWS Management Console access and Programmatic Access via the AWS API, the CLI, and the SDKs.

6. **D** (PCI DSS Level 1)

Explanation:

A PCI DSS Level 1 certification attests to the security of the AWS platform regarding credit card transactions.

7. **A** (AWS Shield)

Explanation:

AWS Shield is AWS' managed DDoS protection service.

8. **B** (AWS Trusted Advisor)

Explanation:

AWS Trusted Advisor can help you assess the fault-tolerance of your AWS environment.

9. **D** (7)

Explanation:

WAF operates down to Layer 7.

10. **B** (AWS Inspector)

Explanation:

AWS Inspector assesses the security and compliance of your EC2 instances.

11. **A** (HIPPA)

Explanation:

A HIPPA certification attests to the fact that the AWS Platform has met the standard required for the secure storage of medical records in the US.

12. **B** (AWS Trusted Advisor)

Explanation:

Trusted Advisor helps you optimize your entire AWS environment in real time following AWS best practices. It helps you optimize cost, fault-tolerance, and more.

13. **C** (Trusted Advisor)

Explanation:

An online resource to help you reduce cost, increase performance, and improve security by optimizing your AWS environment, Trusted Advisor provides real time guidance to help you provision your resources following AWS best practices.

14. **B** (AWS Trusted Advisor)

Explanation:

Trusted Advisor can assist you with the cost optimization of your AWS environment.

15. **C** (Customer data)

Explanation:

The customers are responsible for their own customer data.

16. **B** (All inbound traffic is denied and outbound traffic is allowed by default)

   C (Acts as a virtual firewall to control inbound and outbound traffic)

Explanation:

Security Groups acts as a virtual firewall to control both inbound and outbound traffic. It allows outbound traffic by default and denies all inbound traffic.

17. **D** (Manage services and their capacities)

Explanation:

Feature of AWS Identity and Access Management are:

1. Manage roles and their permissions

2. Manage users and their access

3. Manage federated users and their permissions

18. **B** (Online tool that helps you configure resources to follow best practices)

Explanation:

AWS Trusted Advisor is an online resource for optimizing your AWS environment by following AWS best practices

19. **B** (AWS Management Console Access)

   D (Programmatic Access)

Explanation:

The two types of access that can be granted to a user when creating an IAM policy are:

1. The AWS Management Console

2. Programmatic Access (Command Line Interface and Software Development Kits)

20. **A** (Secure Global Infrastructure)

   B (Meet compliance requirements)

Explanation:

Benefits of AWS Security are:

1. Secure Global Infrastructure

2. Meet compliance requirements

3. Save money

4. Scale quickly

21. **B** (Risk Management)

   C (Control Environment)

   D (Information Security)

Explanation:

AWS Risk and Compliance Program components are:

1. Risk Management

2. Control Environment

3. Information Security

22. B (Delete root user access keys)

Explanation:

Because anyone who has the access key for your AWS account will have unrestricted access to all the resources in your account, including billing information

23. C (Which AWS services are used with the content)

E (In which country the content is stored)

Explanation:

AWS customer maintains ownership and control of their content, including control over:

1. What content they choose to store or process using AWS services

2. Which AWS services they use with their content

3. The AWS Region(s) where their content is stored

4. The format, structure and security of their content, including whether it is masked, anonymised or encrypted

5. Who has access to their AWS accounts and content and how those access rights are granted, managed and revoked

24. A (Laws, Regulations, and Privacy)

E (Certification/Attestations)

Explanation:

AWS Compliance and Assurance Programs include:

1. Certifications / Attestations

2. Laws / Regulations / Privacy

3. Alignments / Frameworks

25. **A** (Security of the cloud)

Explanation:

'Security of the cloud' is the responsibility of AWS, whereas 'Security in the cloud' is customer's responsibility

26. **C** (AWS Enterprise Support)

    D (AWS Trusted Advisor)

Explanation:

AWS provides customers with guidance and expertise through:

1. AWS Trusted Advisor
2. AWS Account Teams
3. AWS Enterprise Support
4. AWS Professional Services and AWS Partner Network
5. AWS Advisories and Bulletins

27. **A** (Only in the perimeter)

Explanation:

Regions, Availability Zones and Edge Locations are a part of the AWS cloud infrastructure

28. **C** (WAF)

Explanation:

AWS WAF is a web application firewall that helps protect your web applications from common web exploits. All the rest of the services mentioned provides fault tolerance.

29. **B** (Identity and Access Management)

Explanation:

IAM controls who is authenticated (signed in) and authorized (has permissions) to use resources

30. **B** (Maintaining physical hardware)

Explanation:

AWS is responsible for protecting the infrastructure that runs all of the services offered in the AWS Cloud. This infrastructure is composed of the hardware, software, networking, and facilities that run AWS Cloud services.

31. **C** (Enable Multi-Factor Authentication)

Explanation:

AWS Multi-Factor Authentication (MFA) is a simple best practice that adds an extra layer of protection on top of your user name and password

32. **B** (False)

Explanation:

It is safer to use IAM roles than it is to use Access Keys.

33. **B** (False)

Explanation:

Identity Access Management is a Global service.

34. **B** (False)

Explanation:

AWS is responsible for the security OF the cloud. The customer is responsible for security IN the cloud -- that is, the security of her AWS resources.

35. **B** (False)

Explanation:

Only AWS Shield Advanced offers automated application layer monitoring.

Chapter 3: Technology

1. **B** (Elastic Load Balancing)

   E (Auto Scaling)

Explanation:

Elastic Load Balancing handles varying loads of traffic by automatically distributing incoming application traffic across multiple targets. Auto Scaling monitors applications and automatically adjusts capacity to maintain steady, predictable performance

2. **A** (Each region is located in a separate geographic area)

   D (Physical location with multiple Availability Zones)

Explanation:

Each region is a separate geographic area and has multiple, isolated locations known as Availability Zones

3. **B** (Distinct locations from within an AWS region that are engineered to be isolated from failures)

Explanation:

Availability Zones are distinct locations from within an AWS region that are engineered to be isolated from failures.

4. **B** (# of Edge Locations > # of Availability Zones > # of Regions)

Explanation:

There are more Availability Zones than Regions and more Edge Locations than Availability Zones.

5. **C** (Glacier)

Explanation:

Glacier offers extremely inexpensive data archival, but requires a 3-5 hour data-retrieval window.

6. **C** (A virtual hard-disk in the cloud)

Explanation:

An EBS volume is best described as a virtual hard-disk in the cloud.

7. **A** (Reserved instances)

Explanation:

Reserved instances are the most economical option for long-term workloads with predictable usage patterns.

8. **B** (Edge Location)

Explanation:

CloudFront content is cached in Edge Locations.

9. **C** (A distinct location within a geographic area designed to provide high availability to a specific geography)

Explanation:

A Region is a distinct location within a geographic area designed to provide high availability to a specific geography.

10. **A** (2)

Explanation:

There are at least 2 Availability Zones per AWS Region.

11. **A** (A resource group is a collection of resources that share one or more tags (or portions of tags)

Explanation:

A resource group is a collection of resources that share one or more tags (or portions of tags.)

12. **A** (On-Demand)

    C (Reserved)

Explanation:

On-Demand and Reserved are the valid EC2 pricing options.

13. **A** (EMR)

Explanation:

Amazon EMR is a web service that makes it easy to process large amounts of data efficiently.

14. **C** (Multi-Region)

Explanation:

A Multi-Region deployment will best ensure global availability.

15. **A** (S3)

Explanation:

With S3, objects can be accessed from anywhere in the world via a dedicated URL.

16. **D** (Aurora)

Explanation:

Aurora is AWS' managed database service that is up to 5X faster than a traditional MySQL database.

17. **D** (A region is a geographical area divided into Availability Zones. Each region contains at least two Availability Zones)

Explanation:

A region is a geographical area divided into Availability Zones. Each region contains at least two Availability Zones.

18. **D** (Redshift)

Explanation:

Redshift is AWS' data warehousing service.

19. **A** (EC2)

   B (Lambda)

Explanation:

EC2 and Lambda are AWS Compute Services.

20. **C** (DMS)

Explanation:

The AWS Database Migrations Service is the best choice.

21. **E** (Moscow)

Explanation:

Moscow is not an AWS Region, while the rest are.

22. **B** (Multiple zones are connected by low latency network links)

   E (A single zone can span multiple data centers)

Explanation:

Multiple, physically separated and isolated Availability Zones are connected with low latency network links that automatically fail-over between one another without interruption. Also a single Availability Zone can span multiple data centers

23. **D** (AWS CloudFront)

Explanation:

AWS CloudFront utilizes edge locations to cache content and reduce latency

24. **D** (Reduces latency)

Explanation:

User requests are served by the closest edge location resulting in reduced latency

25. **D** (Distributes incoming traffic amongst your instances)

Explanation:

Elastic Load Balancing automatically distributes incoming application traffic across multiple targets, such as Amazon EC2 instances, containers, and IP addresses

26. **A** (Latency-based routing)

    B (Geolocation routing)

Explanation:

Amazon Route 53 uses a variety of routing types, including Latency Based Routing, Geo DNS, Geoproximity, and Weighted Round Robin, all of which can be combined with DNS Failover in order to enable a variety of low-latency, fault-tolerant architectures.

27. **D** (Applications with steady state or predictable usage)

Explanation:

Reserved Instances are recommended for applications with steady state or predictable usage as users can commit to a 1-year or 3-year term contract to reduce their total computing costs

28. **B** (AWS Database Migration Service (AWS DMS))

Explanation:

AWS Database Migration Service helps you migrate databases to AWS quickly and securely

29. **D** (AWS Marketplace)

Explanation:

AWS Marketplace is an online store that helps customers find, buy, and immediately start using the software and services they need to build products and run their businesses

30. **D** (Amazon Virtual Private Cloud (Amazon VPC))

Explanation:

Amazon VPC lets you provision a logically isolated section of the AWS cloud where you can launch AWS resources in a virtual network that you define

31. **B** (AWS edge locations)

Explanation:

Amazon CloudFront deliver through a worldwide network of data centers called edge locations

32. **B** (AWS CloudTrail)

Explanation:

CloudTrail logs, continuously monitors, and retains account activity related to actions across your AWS infrastructure

33. **A** (Amazon Simple Notification Service (Amazon SNS))

Explanation:

Amazon Simple Notification Service is a notification service provided as part of Amazon Web Services. It provides a low-cost infrastructure for the mass delivery of messages, predominantly to mobile users

34. **D** (AWS Acceptable Use Policy)

Explanation:

AWS Acceptable Use Policy contains information about prohibited actions on AWS infrastructure

35. **A** (True)

Explanation:

S3 is object storage suitable for the storage of 'flat' files like Word documents, photos, etc.

36. **B** (False)

Explanation:

To restrict access to an entire bucket, you use bucket policies; and to restrict access to an individual object, you use access control lists.

37. **B** (False)

Explanation:

S3 can be used to host *static* websites.

38. **A** (True)

Explanation:

The collection of a CDN's Edge Locations is called a Distribution.

39. **B** (False)

Explanation:

As there are at least two Availability Zones (AZ) per AWS Region, there will always be more AZs than Regions.

40. **B** (False)

Explanation:

Objects stored in S3 are stored in multiple servers in multiple facilities across AWS.

41. **B** (False)

Explanation:

S3 bucket names are global, and must be unique.

42. **A** (True)

Explanation:

A CloudFront Origin can be an S3 bucket, an EC2 instance, an Elastic Load Balancer, or Route 53.

43. **B** (False)

Explanation:

S3 Transfer Acceleration uses AWS' network of Edge Locations to more quickly get your data into AWS.

44. **B** (False)

Explanation:

Bucket Policies are used to make entire buckets (like one hosting an S3 website) public.

Chapter 4: Billing and Pricing

1. **B** (Business)

Explanation:

The Business and Enterprise support plans offer 24 X 7 support via phone or chat.

2. **C** (Basic)

   D (Developer)

   E (Business)

Explanation:

The AWS Support levels are Basic, Developer, Business, and Enterprise.

3. **D** (Enterprise)

Explanation:

Only Enterprise support offers the services of a Technical Account Manager.

4. **B** (20)

Explanation:

The default maximum is 20 linked accounts. This soft limit can be increased by contacting AWS.

5. **B** (Developer)

Explanation:

The Developer support plan features access to AWS support during business hours via email.

6. **D** (Reserved instances)

Explanation:

EC2 Reserved Instances offer significant discounts for a contracted term-of-service.

7. **A** (VPC)

 E (Auto-Scaling)

 F (Elastic Beanstalk)

 G (CloudFormation)

 J (IAM)

Explanation:

The correct answers are VPC, Elastic Beanstalk, CloudFormation, IAM, and Auto-Scaling. Please keep in mind that with VPC, Elastic Beanstalk, CloudFormation, and Auto-Scaling, the underlying provisioned resources will incur charges.

8. **D** (Business)

Explanation:

Both the Business and Enterprise support levels offer a < 4-hour response time in the event of an impaired production system.

9. **A** (Additional storage)

 D (Clock hours of server time)

 E (Number of requests)

Explanation:

Clock hours of server time, additional storage, and number of requests are among the criteria defining charges for RDS.

10. **A** (Data-in)

Explanation:

In AWS, data-in is always free-of-charge.

11. **A** (CloudWatch)

Explanation:

A CloudWatch alarm can be set to monitor spending on your AWS Account.

12. **B** (Billing support)

Explanation:

All accounts receive billing support.

13. **D** (The Dev team will be billed for two instances at on-demand prices and two instances at the reserved instance price)

Explanation:

Assuming all instances are in the same AWS Organization, the reserved instance pricing for the unused QA instances will be applied to two of the four Dev instances.

14. **B** (Business)

   C (Enterprise)

Explanation:

Both Enterprise and business support plans feature unlimited (customer-side) contacts and unlimited support cases.

15. **A** (Spot instances)

Explanation:

Spot instances would be the most cost-effective solution.

16. **B** (Number of hours Elastic Load Balancer runs)

   D (Number of instances)

Explanation:

Factors that need to be considered for Amazon EC2 pricing are:

   1. Clock Hours of Server Time

   2. Machine Configuration

   3. Machine Purchase Type

4. Number of Instances

5. Load Balancing

6. Detailed Monitoring

7. Auto Scaling

8. Elastic IP Addresses

9. Operating Systems and Software Packages

17. **C** (AWS Web Application Firewall (WAF))

Explanation:

AWS WAF also follows the 'pay only for what you use' model and is not free.

18. **E** (Total Cost of Ownership (TCO) calculator)

Explanation:

AWS Total Cost of Ownership (TCO) Calculator provides a comparative analysis of the cost estimation by comparing on premises and co-location environments to the AWS.

19. **B** (Input Output Operations per Seconds (IOPS))

Explanation:

When estimating the cost of Amazon S3, the following are considered:

1. Storage Class

2. Storage (Number and size of objects)

3. Requests

4. Data Transfer

20. **D** (Access to Well-Architected Review delivered by AWS Solution Architects)

Explanation:

Access to Well-Architected Review delivered by AWS Solution Architects is available only for Enterprise customers

AWS Certified Cloud Practitioner

21. **D** (One primary contact may open a case)

    E (Business hours access to Cloud Support Associates via email)

Explanation:

24/7 access to Cloud Support Engineers via email, chat, and phone and Unlimited contacts opening a case is available to Business and Enterprise customers, whereas Technical Account Manager is only available with Enterprise support plan.

22. **A** (Economies of scale)

Explanation:

Economies of scale results in the transfer of savings back to the customer in the form of lower pricing.

23. **A** (Inbound data transfer across all Amazon Web Services in all regions)

    E (Outbound data transfer between Amazon Web Services within the same region)

Explanation:

While Data Transfer Out comes with a price, there is no charge for inbound data transfer across all Amazon Web Services in all regions. In addition, there are no outbound data transfer charges between Amazon Web Services within the same region.

24. **B** (False)

Explanation:

The Paying Account cannot make changes to any of the resources owned by a Linked Account.

25. **A** (True)

Explanation:

With AWS Organizations, you can use either just the Consolidated Billing feature, or all the offered features.

Note from the Author:

Reviews are gold to authors! If you have enjoyed this book and helped you along certification, would you consider rating it and reviewing it?

Link to Product Page: